ALAN RANGER

Würzburg radar
& Mobile 24kVA Generator

Published in Poland in 2019
by Wydawnictwo Stratus sp.j.
Żeromskiego 4,
27-600 Sandomierz 1, Poland
e-mail: office@wydawnictwostratus.pl

as
MMPBooks
e-mail: office@mmpbooks.biz

© Wydawnictwo Stratus sp.j.
© 2019 MMPBooks
© Alan Ranger

www.mmpbooks.biz
www.wydawnictwostratus.pl

ISBN
978-83-65958-53-2

Editor in chief
Roger Wallsgrove

Editorial Team
Bartłomiej Belcarz
Robert Pęczkowski
Artur Juszczak

Cover concept
Dariusz Grzywacz

Book layout
Dariusz Grzywacz

All photos: author's collection except stated

DTP
Wydawnictwo Stratus sp.j.

PRINTED IN POLAND

Foreword

In this series of books, I have no intention of trying to add to what is already a very well documented history of Germany's anti-aircraft defence systems, and their associated radar systems as it has been covered by previous publications. Here I hope to give an impression through original photographs, taken both during and before war, of the *Würzburg* Radar system and its crews, as well as the electrical generators that supplied the power for them, in all the various theatres of operation they found themselves operating in.

Here in this publication I hope to show what was seen through the lens of the normal German soldier's camera, the soldiers that had to live with and operate these systems each and every day, not the professional PK cameramen whose well posed and sanitized shots are well known and have been published over and over again. As such they have been seen by most interested parties by now already, however the images taken by individual soldiers show a more personal view of the radar systems and their installations that the soldiers both lived and worked in, the

This photograph shows, in the foreground, a *Freya* radar operating around 2.4 m (125 MHz) with 15-kW peak power giving it a range of some 130 km. The basic *Freya* radar was continuously improved, with over 1,000 systems eventually built. In the background is a *Würzburg-Riese* radar (Giant *Würzburg*). It had a 7.5m (25-foot) dish (manufactured by Zeppelin). The system used increased transmitter power and this, combined with the enlarged reflector dish, resulted in it having a range of up to 70 km, as well as greatly increased accuracy. In all about 1,500 of this type of radar system were built.

views that interested the common soldier not the professional propagandist. For the most part these photographs have been in private collections and have only recently come onto the market.

Most images we have used here were taken from prints made on old German Agfa paper stock and the majority of these original prints are no more than 25 mm by 45 mm in size. Whilst we have used the best quality photos from my collection, occasionally due to the interesting or the rare nature of the subject matter a photo of a lesser quality has been included.

History

The history of radar is like many other recent technological innovations that originated in the first half of the 20th century. A period in our history where the co-operation between nations was virtually non-existent and, especially between the European powers, a spirit of mistrust prevailed. Like many other inventions of the time, the invention of radar was a development being worked on in parallel by many nations in complete secrecy, such that no one nation knew of the other's work on the subject and each claimed the invention as their own.

In Germany, radar was being worked on from 1928 primarily by a team lead by Professor Hans E. Hollmann who, in 1927 whilst working for the University of Darmstadt, had invented and developed a working ultra-short wave transmitter and receiver for both centimetre and decimetre waves. A fellow scientist by the name of Dr Hans-Karl von Willisen who was also working with ultra-short wave technology befriended Hollmann and the two became firm friends and started a company, along with a businessman named Paul Günther Erbslöh. The company was named GEMA (*Gesellschaft für elektroakustische und mechanische Apparate*). Erbsloeh managed the firm while Hollmann and von Willisen handled product development. In 1934 GEMA released their first product, a shipborne radar for detecting other shipping. This radar operated on the 50 cm wave length using *Braunschen* tubes (*Braunsche Röhre*). It was named *Seetakt* (*Seetaktisch*) and was capable of locating vessels up to 10 kilometres away. By the summer of 1935 they had developed the radar further, such that in a demonstration to the German navy they managed to locate the battleship *Königsberg* at a distance of 8 kilometres with an accuracy of within 50 meters. The Germans attempted to produce a magnetron that would have improved their results immeasurably, but they never managed to stabilize their design, unlike the British who with that technology stole the march on Germany in the years to come. However the *Seetakt* radar technology was further developed and fine-tuned. A wavelength of 60 to 80 cm was used,

Here we have a FuMG 64 *Mannheim* (radar) which was a development of the earlier 'Mainz' radar. It had a 3-meter reflector, which was made from a lattice framework covered in a fine mesh. This was fixed to the front of a control cabin and the whole apparatus was rotated electrically.

This photo is also of a FuMG 64 *Mannheim*. Its range was 25–35 km, with an accuracy of ±10–15 meters, and azimuth and elevation accuracy of ±0.15 degrees. Although the type was accurate enough to control Flak guns, it was not deployed in large numbers due mostly to its cost. This was about 3 times as much in both time and materials to manufacture than the FuMG 62 *Würzburg*.

which enabled the transmitter and receiver unit to be placed closer together in order to achieve the location of an aircraft at a height of 5,000 meters and 28 kilometres distant. This-land-based aircraft location system was named *Freya* and with this development GEMA had both radar systems on the market by the end of 1935.

In Germany at this time, a major company already established in the electronics industry was Telefunken, and they had taken note of Hollmann's development work in the field of radar. As early as 1933 they started research of their own but no great impetus had been given to their efforts. However, with a viable product entering the market Telefunken stepped up the project's priority and in late 1936 they were putting the final touches to a radar they had developed under the project title of the FuMG 39T *Darmstadt*. This was given the name *Würzburg* once a finished product was ready to market. The *Würzburg* worked on a 53 cm wavelength and utilized a 3 metre diameter parabolic dish antenna with a rotating dipole. This system had an operating range of 10 kilometres with an accuracy of within 100 metres in distance and azimuth, and elevation accuracy of 0.25°. After a demonstration of the *Würzburg* to Ernst Udet, who at the time was director of research and development of the German *Luftwaffe*, the *Luftwaffe* started to place orders for the *Würzburg* radar system, which by 1937 had been improved by having its range increased.

The *Luftwaffe* recognised the advantages of both the *Würzburg* and *Freya* systems, and realized that by pairing the two systems in one location they would have the ability to spot and track aircraft at distance using the *Freya* and then as they got closer using the *Würzburg* they could determine the aircraft's exact range and height. They would be able to direct a fighter to intercept any incoming threat. In 1939 the combination of these two systems gave the Germans the best radar system in the world at the time. It was both mobile and far more accurate than the British "Chain Home" static radar system, but the fact that the Germans did not have the backup manual data management systems in place meant that they did not manage to use the system to its full advantage, unlike the British who used their radar system to the full and arguably it played a most important part in winning the Battle of Britain during the summer of 1940.

Another system that was developed in Germany and entered service in 1942 was the FuMG 64 *Mannheim* radar. It was also paired up with *Würzburg* in operation and was by far superior to the *Freya*. However it never fully replaced the *Freya* due to the *Mannheim* being very complicated to manufacture and the amount of key resources it took to produce. The number of CRTs (cathode ray tubes) that it took to make was nearly double that of a *Würzburg* unit. It simply proved too expensive to manufacture in large numbers.

As the war progressed the Germans did manage the use of their radar systems better, setting up systems such as the *Himelbeck* early warning system that took a terrible toll upon the men and aircraft involved in the Allied bombing offensive. It was only partially countered by the British inventing the countermeasure of dropping "Window" (later known as Chaff), as the Germans soon realised that the effect of Window could be negated by changing the wavelength that the radars operated on. It could be said that this was the very start of electronic warfare.

Development & Introduction

The FuMG 62 *Würzburg* went through a series of major developments that resulted in a number of different variants being manufactured. The initial model, the *Würzburg* A, required the operator to manually tune the signal so that the oscilloscope (a type of cathode ray tube) display lined up the target, but the system suffered from interference so it was required to operate with an attached searchlight system. When a rough location of an aircraft could determined, the searchlights would pin-point its location. Despite this unit's limitation, it was responsible for the first German radar victory when, in May of 1940, with only the radar operator giving verbal directions to a Flak unit, a bomber was shot down.

The next variant of the *Würzburg* was the model B, very similar to the model A but it had an additional infra-red detector incorporated into its system. This was supposed to aid fine tuning and increase the accuracy of the unit, but in the field this additional system proved unsuitable and production of the model B was rapidly cancelled.

With the cancellation of the model B, the model C was rushed into production. It utilized a lobe switching device to improve accuracy. The system was fitted with two slightly off-centre transmitter poles located in the antenna dish, and by switching the transmission's signal rapidly between the two poles the returning pulses off each would differ slightly due to the different location of their origination. By tuning the system so that the two pulsing signal lobes matched in height on the screen, the location of the target could be accurately gauged. This system was both more accurate and faster than all its predecessors.

The last major change to the *Würzburg* came with the model D that entered service in 1941. This model was fitted with a conical scanning system that utilized an offset signal receiver that was given the code name of *Quirl* that in German translates to whisk. The *Quirl* was mounted on a pole located in the centre on the parabolic dish and spun around, so that signal it generated when returned grew in strength dependent upon which side of the centreline's axis the target's reflected signal came from. Thus the dish could be moved to follow the target. This system also resulted in the angular resolution of the returning signal being smaller than the beam width of the receiving antenna, resulting in huge improvement in accuracy such that azimuth results were within 0.2° and elevation was improved to within 0.3°.

As all the variants of the *Würzburg* used the same dish and electrical enclosures, it was possible to upgrade all previous models of the *Würzburg* to model D standard by replacing electrical panels inside the cabinets and the mounting of the *Quirl* to the 3 metre parabolic dish.

Following the development described above, the *Würzburg* had reached the limit of its development. It was still not considered accurate enough to direct accurate gun fire without assistance from other systems, such as searchlights. The *Luftwaffe* realized that a new radar system was required that could operate independently. This requirement was eventually met by the introduction of the FuMG 65 *Würzburg Riese* radar system.

The *Würzburg* radar system as was previously mentioned was a portable system. In order to facilitate its mobility, the 3 metre parabolic dish was split into two halves along its horizontal axis and was able to be folded in half for transportation. Originally it was produced and mounted on a cruciform base identical to that fitted to many other items of German military equipment, such as its own electrical 24 volt generator, the 3.7 cm Flak 18 and the *Richtungshörer* (RRH) sound ranging device amongst many other items. This cruciform base was designed so that it could be hooked up to the Sd.Anh. 104 twin bogie transportation equipment and then be towed by any suitable motorized vehicle. The *Würzburg* radar system was also mounted on a rectangular 4-wheel trailer base that was fitted with stabilizers at each corner. These were folded up for transportation and down when the unit was to be set into a new operating location. This trailer also needed to be towed by a suitable motorized vehicle.

As an end note it is of interest to mention that the *Seetakt* radar first came into British hands following the scuttling of the German pocket-battleship *Admiral Graff Spee* outside the harbour of Montevideo. The ship settled to the bottom but the aerial masts and gunnery control house were still above water, and were recovered by the Royal Navy for evaluation. A *Würzburg* radar system was identified and located in operation at the French cliff-top village of Bruneval, just north of the French port of Le Havre, and a Commando raid named "Operation Bellicose" was organised. It was a huge success, with major parts of the radar system and even one of the operators captured, and all taken back to Britain for evaluation and interrogation.

Electrical generators used with German radar units

The German radar units were supplied with the necessary electrical generators, all of which had to be able to supply 24-kilowatts, usually based around a 51-horsepower (38 kW) 8-cylinder engine, giving a current of 200 amperes at 110 volts. Whilst many manufacturers' types were used, in particularly when a radar unit was to be installed as part of a long-term static location such as being installed as part of the Atlantic Wall defensive system, when a radar unit was to be mobile either one of two types were almost exclusively issued. One predominated in the early stages of the war and another later replaced it. The first mobile electrical generator issued utilized the same cruciform base and associated Sd.Anh. 104 transportation equipment as the *Würzburg* radar unit itself, but the later type electrical generator was fitted with its own two-wheel "U" shaped trailer frame. Whilst in both cases the generator could be removed from their base plate or frame it was a rare occurrence. In most cases, when a temporary location was set up the equipment would be protected by ground works. These would be formed by the crews digging trenches running from one element to another and building circular embankments around each individual element of the radar unit with the spoil from the trenches.

A *Luftwaffe* unit is seen here passing through a German town in December of 1942. The Krupp L3H163 truck in the lead is towing a 51-horsepower (38 kW) 8-cylinder diesel engine used to drive an electrical generator that could produce a current of 200 amperes at 110 volts.

Other elements of the *Luftwaffe*'s ground defence

The *Luftwaffe*'s ground defence was made up from many parts. Flak weapons were but the active components, in order to form a comprehensive defence and ensure its effectiveness many other elements were required. The *Luftwaffe* used many mechanical and optical devices, at the tip of their technical advancement was the radar but other pieces of equipment played their part, key amongst them were the following that I have included in this publication in order to give perspective to the radar that is the subject of this book. I do intend to produce a publication on the *Luftwaffe*'s ground equipment but this will be subject to the time I have left to write it.

This photograph is of a *Doppelfernrohr* (double telescope) 10x80 *Flakfernrohr*. In 1936 Emil Busch AG of Rathenow won the *Luftwaffe* contract with their design, chosen for its light weight and wide field of view that were both better than all other designs under consideration. Busch began production immediately after the contract was awarded and production continued until the war's end, with many sub-contractors throughout Europe building licensed copies as well. The unit featured the following optical dimensions: 80 mm cemented achromatic objectives with 280 mm focal length, 70° eyepieces fitted with 45° Schmidt prisms.

Another photo of a *Doppelfernrohr* 10x80 *Flakfernrohr*. Of note here is the rough sight frame that was fitted to the top of the unit, to enable the user to target the aircraft before coping with the magnification of the sight that could make it hard to find a moving target quickly.

Above: Pictured here in a Flak emplacement is this crewman using an EM34 or EM36 *Entfernungsmesser* 1 m Range Finder fitted to a shoulder support frame. The Range Finder worked using the coincidence of image principal of triangulation, where by moving the two images of the target received from the two lenses, one at each end of the range finder, until they overlapped and became one. Then via the mathematics of trigonometry the range (distance) to the target could be worked out. This was achieved by an internal sliding scale fitted to the unit and the range could be read off the graticule through the eye piece and called out to the gunner.

Left: This photo is of a *Kinotheodolite*, a specialized type of theodolite that was usually emplaced with a fixed flak battery. The unit would be placed on either a permanent pedestal or tripod so that the horizontal level could be fixed permanently. The *Kinotheodolite* was essentially a type of telescope with integrated crosshairs, a vertical and a horizontal sub circle with several graduations which actually served to align the device to the correct orientation. The readings were then fed electrically into an electromechanical computer that gave an accurate reading of both height and distance to the target.

Another soldier is pictured here sitting whilst using a EM34 or EM36 *Entfernungsmesser* 1 m Range Finder. One of the lenses of this stereoscopic range finder is clearly visible here at the end of the range finder, the padded end cap was purely a device to help reduce damage to the unit during handling.

Seen here mounted on steel pedestal is this *Kinotheodolite* and in this view its associated electromechanical computer is clearly visible.

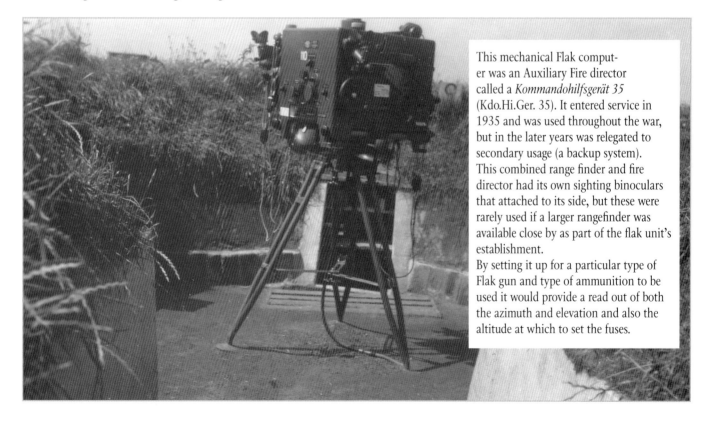

This mechanical Flak computer was an Auxiliary Fire director called a *Kommandohilfsgerät 35* (Kdo.Hi.Ger. 35). It entered service in 1935 and was used throughout the war, but in the later years was relegated to secondary usage (a backup system). This combined range finder and fire director had its own sighting binoculars that attached to its side, but these were rarely used if a larger rangefinder was available close by as part of the flak unit's establishment.

By setting it up for a particular type of Flak gun and type of ammunition to be used it would provide a read out of both the azimuth and elevation and also the altitude at which to set the fuses.

This Kdo.Hi.Ger. 35 is set up without its own optics but is being used in conjunction with its attendant *Entfernungsmesser* R(H) 34 or 36, (EM R(H) 34/36) rangefinder instead. The Kdo.Hi.Ger. 35 had its own bespoke trailer, the Sd.Anh. 53. It was a two wheel box type trailer that opened from the rear and the Kdo.Hi.Ger. 35 was fitted onto a sliding tray and was then pushed into the box body of the trailer for transportation.

Another view of the Kdo.Hi.Ger. 35 being paired with a EM R(H) 34/36, but the the focus of attention of the picture is on the EM R(H) 34/36. The EM R(H) 34 entered service in 1934 and was updated in 1936 to the EM R(H) 36. This only differed by having a thermally-activated compensation device fitted internally that automatically compensated for the thermal expansion of the tubular housing that otherwise would have had an effect on the device's readings.

This photograph of a flak position on the cliffs near the French port of Boulogne clearly shows us the working of the control system for the battery of four 88 mm Flak guns. In the foreground we see the EM R(H) 34/36 with the Kdo.Hi.Ger. 35 behind it and then, behind the accommodation bunkers for the gun crews, is one of the 88 mm Flak guns they serve.

Here we have a *Kommandogerät* 36 (Kdo.Ger. 36) Fire Control System, a state of the art electromechanical computing device that worked in conjunction with the EM R(H) 40 optical rangefinder. Kdo.Ger. 36 could be programmed with the projectile weight, the powder temperature and dampness, the gun barrel's condition, projectile drift, barometric pressure, wind speed and wind direction. All these values were ascertained two or more times a day and were among the usual duties associated with a Flak crew.

Another view of a different Kdo.Ger. 36 beautifully emplaced with the use of rattan work and a soil bund. The two crew members are feeding in the latest environmental figures obtained to keep the device prepared for immediate use, and are being photographed by an official photographer, whilst he in turn is being photographed by a member of the Flak crew.

This is a *Ringtrichter Richtungshörer Horchgerät* (RRH) that translates from German as Funnel Ring Sound Locator. This type of sound locating technology had been around since before the first world war and was in use by most industrialised nations, but by the 1940s reached the end of its useful development. Amongst the world's many different systems it is widely agreed that the German RRH, as seen here, was the very apex of this design technology. It boasted an obtainable accuracy of +/ – 2° in both the horizontal and vertical planes, however beyond 5 kilometres and out to a maximum of 12 kilometres these results were very dependent on good stable weather conditions. These devices would no doubt have faded from front line service as the war progressed but by a strange quirk of fate their services became invaluable again once the Allies started to use jamming technology such as "Window" against German's electronic location systems. This ensured the RRH would be in service right up until the war's end.

Another RRH being used whilst set up in a wheat field in the summer of 1941. Of note are the rain covers for the crew that, whilst fitted, have been rolled up on top of their support frame to act as a sun shield for the operators, whom I guess felt it was not such a bad day to be in the *Luftwaffe*. Note here the one half of an Sd.Anh. 104 twin bogie transportation system seen at the far right of the page. Like many other *Luftwaffe* devices the RRH was transported by the use of this ubiquitous yet usually overlooked piece of German equipment.

Amongst the many types of searchlights used by the German armed forces during WW2 was the 150 cm *Flakscheinwerfer type 37* (150 cm Sw 37). This one is seen pre-war still in its three-colour Reichswehr camouflage of Dark Green, Red Brown and Earth-Yellow. The system had a detection range of about 8 kilometres (5.0 miles) for targets at an altitude of between 4,000 and 5,000 metres (13,000 and 16,000 ft). It was mounted in a frame that gave it 360° rotation and an elevation of up to 90° and had an illumination equivalent to 1,200 million candlepower. It used 200 amps, 110 volts, 34 kW, usually provided by a mobile generator. Note yet again the use of the Sd.Anh. 104 twin bogie system.

This photograph depicts a 200 cm Sw 40, another of the standard searchlights used by the *Luftwaffe*. This larger searchlight used 450 amps, 110 volts, 60 kW that was supplied by a custom Messerschmitt generator that was supplied with the unit. The more powerful 200 cm light was often used in conjunction with radar and acted as the lead light for a unit of the standard 150 cm Sw 37s. The 200 cm Sw 40 was made mobile by the use of the Sd.Anh. 204 twin bogie system that was essentially the same as the Sd.Anh. 104, but larger and able to take more weight.

The third of the three most common types of German searchlight was the 60 cm Sw 36. It used an 8 kW generator and produced a light beam with the equivalent to 135 million candlepower. This small searchlight was usually associated with either the 20 mm light or 37 mm medium Flak units and utilized the same trailer for its mobility as the 20 mm Flak guns, the Sd.Anh. 51 type. The 60 cm Sw 36 also utilized the same triangular base plate as the Flak 30 was mounted on.

Würzburg Radar

This good quality photograph is of an early model FuMG 62 *Würzburg* that has been updated to type "D" standard. It gives us a great view of the crew in their operating positions working the unit. Note the calibration indicator dials on the side of the locator's scope control box.

This model "A" FuMG 62 *Würzburg* is seen being set up in a field outside the city limits of Darmstadt a few kilometres south of Frankfurt. Of most interest here is the early style platform trailer that the unit is mounted on. Although this type of trailer was still in use at the end of the war, due to the constant upgrading of the radar unit mounted upon it they did become a rarity by the war's end. However it just happens that the one FuMG 62 unit on public display in the UK is of this early type.

This photo is at the other end of the scale from the photo above. It's taken in November 1943 in the winter wasteland of the Russian steppes close to a captured Russian airfield used by the *Luftwaffe* near Veshka, close to the western shore of Lake Ilmen. Visible in the photograph are two *Würzburg* FuMG 62 model "D" radars in their earthwork emplacements and the associated accommodation for the crews.

This well-established site is located on the Baltic coast and whilst these radar units do serve as part of the German air defence network, the real reason for their location was to track the flight path of the "V" weapons during firing tests over that region of the coast. Not many units were set up in such permanent or well established locations. The two types of radar on show here are in the distance a *Würzburg-Riese* radar (The Giant *Würzburg*) and in the foreground an early type model "A" FuMG 62 *Würzburg* mounted on the early rectangular platform. But as it's been there a while, the crew have built an extended circular timber plank platform around it to make operating the unit easier. It looks like these units have been there for a long time and they have, but foliage like that grown around the FuMG 62 could have grown in only a matter of two to three months during spring.

Opposite page: This 1944 photo of a radar unit on the move shows a *Würzburg* FuMG 62 model "D" radar loaded on a railway flatbed on the move to its next location. Note that by the late summer of 1944 the operating crew has already been stripped of its older crew members and only technical senior staff remain. The other tasks are now taken up by children recruited directly from the Hitler Youth, such was the strain on manpower in the German armed forces late in the war.

Both the photos on top of this page are of a model "D" FuMG 62 *Würzburg* dish converted for fitting to a permanent structure that was also collapsible, such that during storms the dish could be lowered into a protective enclosure to protect it from wind damage. Located on the Norwegian coast, this Model "D" unit is also fitted with a variation of the IFF system (Identification Friend or Foe), the FuG 25 *Zwilling*. Its inclusion in this system is witnessed by the twin dipoles mounted here on the upper edge of the radar dish.

Bottom: This photo is of a similar *Würzburg* system as seen above but is a different unit. This one is located on the north sea coast and is based on the German island of Sylt. Again the IFF is fitted to this unit and also visible in this view is the counter-weight that made the unit more balanced and therefore more stable when raised and in operation.

Here we have a close-up of the *Würzburg* radar dish seen on the bottom of page 20. The IFF aerial dipoles are clearly visible here as is the detail of the counterbalance system for the dish. Also clear in this view are the reinforcement braces fitted to the rear of the dish on either side, to ensure that this flimsy metal dish is not damaged by the severe weather conditions common to the island of Sylt.

Below: This model "A" FuMG 62 *Würzburg* is seen whilst its crew are erecting an elaborate camouflage screen around it. The use of netting as opposed to using timber walls is due to the carbon in the wood having a hugely adverse effect on the performance of the radar unit. Often a barn-like structure that was collapsible was created around a unit, but it had to be lowered before the radar became affective. The use of netting meant that this unit can operate as it is currently situated, obscured from view by the netting but without any interference to the signal.

This radar unit is located inland from the Pas de Calais, France, and it can be seen that it should be considered a permanent emplacement. This unit is photographed here in the summer of 1943. It is just such locations that were among those that received attention from the Organization Todt and became a concrete fortification incorporated in to what became known as the Atlantic Wall. This site has both a FuMG 62 *Würzburg* and a FuMG 64 *Mannheim* working in co-operation with each other.

Below: A radar unit based on the Cherbourg Peninsular close to the town of Valognes. The crews of the various items of *Luftwaffe* equipment based here are having a summer picnic to celebrate mid-summers day 1943. As well as the FuMG 62 *Würzburg* in the background, seen here complete with kill markings on its dish are an RRH listening unit and a FuMG 64 *Mannheim* as well as a searchlight unit, all visible in other photos in this set. Unfortunately the soldier who took the photos was no professional and sadly most of his photos are woefully out of focus and as such unprintable.

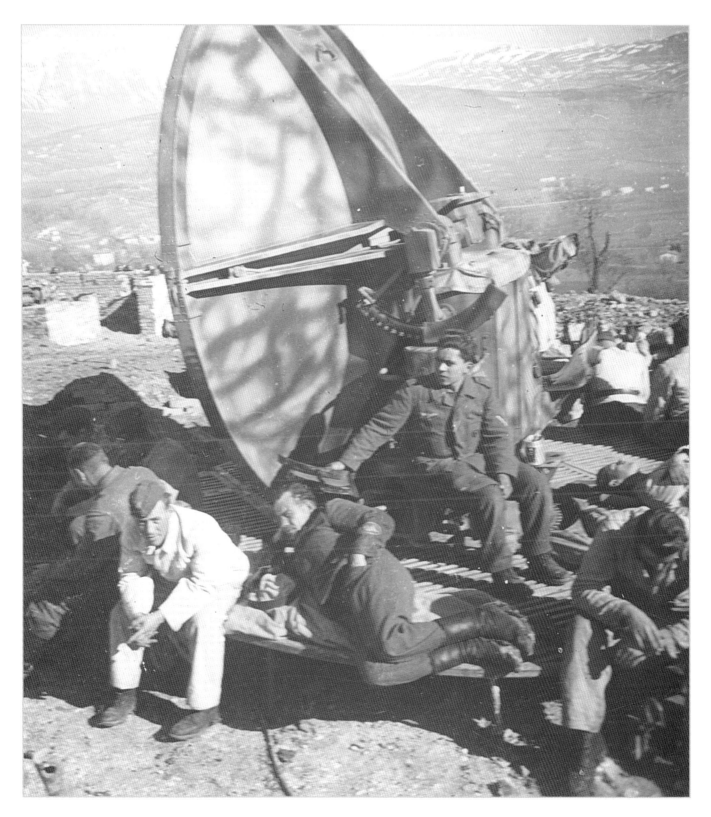

This photograph is of a radar unit equipped with a model "D" FuMG 62 *Würzburg* set up on the veranda of a mountaintop villa in central Italy in the late summer of 1943. The unit is relaxed and seated awaiting a mail call, a welcome distraction from their daily routine. In the clarity of this photograph the intricate camouflage paint job on the radar unit can be seen. It is light Green over Dark Yellow, a fairly common colour combination in the Italian theatre of operations. Also of note here are the foldable wooded floor panels that folded up, one each side of the central segment, during transportation.

"Bring on the rain" – here we have an FuMG 62 *Würzburg* radar set up with full wet weather protection fitted. These factory produced rain covers for the crew to operate under did not last long in service and it is common to see blankets and other material used as temporary replacement rain covers. This photo also offers us a good view of the rear of the radar from outside its protective mud-walled emplacement.

A model "D" FuMG 62 *Würzburg* set up on the top of a single storey wooden Flak tower somewhere close to the Dutch coast in the autumn of 1943. Raised towers such as this served two purposes in Holland – keeping the electrically operated equipment out of the wet and often flooded fields and better signal reception. Reception was improved when a unit was located above the ground away from ground clutter, houses, trees and other obstacles in the line of sight of the radar signal that produced interference. Note the 6 kill markings painted on the radar dish and the protective cover placed over the *Quirl* located on the end of the pole that projects from the centre of the radar's dish.

This model "A" FuMG 62 *Würzburg* that has both been updated to model "D" specifications, and also fitted with an IFF system, is seen having just arrived at its new operating position. A safety line has been put in place to prevent the unit being blown over and also to reduce rocking whilst the four stabilization frames that drop down, one from each corner, are set up to level the operation platform. The timber will be used to assist in making a level platform for the unit. Note the *Quirl* has not been screwed onto the central rod and the IFF dipole rods have not yet been installed either. The young crewman with his rifle slung uncomfortably over his shoulder is seen holding onto one of the four stabilisation frame screw jacks that has yet to be fixed into position. Of note are the Dark Green lines painted over the Dark Grey base colour on both halves of the dish, that look to have been painted whilst the two halves were in their folded down position.

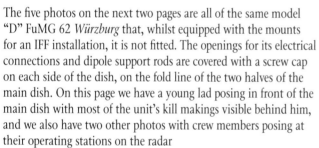

The five photos on the next two pages are all of the same model "D" FuMG 62 *Würzburg* that, whilst equipped with the mounts for an IFF installation, it is not fitted. The openings for its electrical connections and dipole support rods are covered with a screw cap on each side of the dish, on the fold line of the two halves of the main dish. On this page we have a young lad posing in front of the main dish with most of the unit's kill makings visible behind him, and we also have two other photos with crew members posing at their operating stations on the radar

On this page we have two more photos from this unit. At the top we have another young member of the crew posing in front of the main dish with the rain cover over the *Quirl*, the bottom photograph shows a number of the old hands posing in the radar's emplacement. This photo offers us a clue as to how this emplacement was constructed; it looks like the side retaining walls are made from timber boards recycled from old storage boxes and shipping crates.

Above: Here we can see a pair of *Luftwaffe* officers photographed inspecting the installation. Obviously a relaxed atmosphere exits here as in my experience inspections were never so frivolous and light-hearted, although in hindsight many should have been.

A nice profile view of a model "D" FuMG 62 *Würzburg* emplaced in the hills above the French port of La Rochelle. Whilst the unit is unmanned it obviously ready for action as all the covers have been removed and items such as the central *Quirl* are clearly visible.

This is a nice photograph of a FuMG 62 *Würzburg* having its covers pulled into place by its crew in preparation for its next move to a new operating position. Note the Sd.Anh. 104 twin bogie transportation system in place and the towing beam raised, ready to be hitched to its assigned towing vehicle

A model "D" FuMG 62 *Würzburg* and its crew photographed on Christmas Day 1944 in northern Holland. With the Allies advancing upon their position I doubt many more peaceful days were to be had for this crew. The radar has the new updated *Quirl* that had a built-in IFF system so the old mounting points for the system are left in their covered state, never to be used again. Of note are the two white painted silhouettes of British 4-engined bombers that represent kills to date for the unit.

The same crew at the same radar location, but in this view the radar has been rotated through 180° and is now viewed from the rear. Christmas cheer has taken hold here and a happy atmosphere is self-evident.

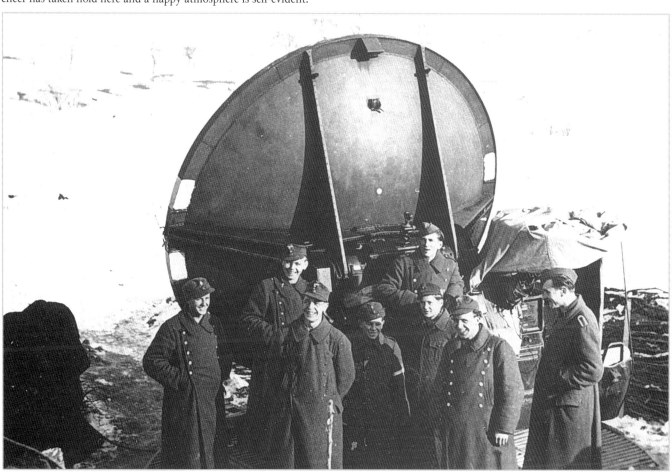

This model "A" FuMG 62 *Würzburg* has been recently set up on the Belgian coast near Ostend, with sand being used to form the protective emplacement bund walls and fishing nets being used to hide the set's location from the seaward side only. Of interest here is the barrage balloon in the background, a rarity in the German inventory. Although not impossible for this balloon to be German, it is more likely to be one left behind by the British following their retreat and eventual evacuation from close by Dunkirk.

A radar unit set up in the grounds of Calais municipal campsite. The nicely laid down footpaths are the most established part of the site; the radar has literally been set up in the sand dunes. This actual location did not change over the next couple of years, but the amount of concrete poured on this beach changed its appearance for ever. Many of the bunkers built here by the Germans still exist today, this part of the French coast is literally covered in them and has been permanently changed.

Photographed in the autumn of 1943, a few young members of the crew of this model "D" FuMG 62 *Würzburg* pose for a snap to send home. Clear in this photo are the hinge lines that indicate where the wooden operating platform floor folds are, and the wet weather cover for the main operator that has seen better days. Whilst one of the long slits up the canvas is the doorway, the other is just a tear.

This is a training session and demonstration for local young recruits with the FuMG 62 *Würzburg* in the background. It shows them using an EM R(H) 34/36 rangefinder that is also in service on the site, which is on the hill overlooking the Rhine river valley. Just visible in the far distance is a castle that is built on top of a hill on the other side of the river.

Here we have a close-up of the radar site that was first seen on the top of page 30. In this closer view we can see that the radar has had a wooden retaining wall built and then has had sand piled up against it to provide a level of protection for the operating crew. The camouflage that has been fashioned out of wooden poles from which fishing nets have been hung probably did serve it purpose well from the sea, but from the air or from inland the radar unit was still easily identifiable. In the foreground we can see that the crew are cultivating sunflowers – I am not sure of their significance, if indeed they have any, but I have other photos from different units that are seen to be growing sunflowers as well. Lastly of note is the radar dish itself that has the upgraded *Quirl* with the built-in IFF and also the dish still has the old installation points for the dipole mounting rods for the now redundant FuG 25 *Zwilling* IFF set. They are left covered, unused, with their steel caps screwed on.

Opposite page: This is the same radar as seen in the bottom photograph on page 31, but in this photograph we see the C/O posing with the site's *Doppelfernrohr* 10x80 *Flakfernrohr* sighting scope. The rest of the crew are lined up on parade behind him. Of note are the two crew immediately to the left behind the C/O – one looks to be of school age whilst the other with the pipe in his mouth is probably in his 50's.

This is a good photograph of a working radar site. The groundwork is all new, as demonstrated by the total lack of weed growth on the recently dug soil. This emplacement contains both the *Kommandogerät* 36 (Kdo.Ger. 36) Fire Control System and the FuMG 62 *Würzburg*. From a generator that is just out of our picture come the power cables, laid in the small trench in the foreground. The pole in the centre of the emplacement is being used to raise a power cable above a piece of rotating equipment that needs power fed to it from the top, to enable it to rotate without the cable winding around its base.

Below: This early model "D" FuMG 62 *Würzburg* has its improved version of the *Quirl* mounted on the centre support pole but it does not yet have the IFF upgrade. So the original FuG 25 IFF radio set still requires the twin dipoles mounted on their support rods, that are screwed into their location mounts close to the outer edge of the main radar receiver dish. In this view we can see some of the folding supports for the fold-down operator's platform and also we can see that this site has either only just been set up or is in a place where a protective emplacement is not considered necessary.

A great group portrait of *Luftwaffe* personnel with a late model "D" FuMG 62 *Würzburg* in the background. This radar unit has the late up-graded *Quirl* with the IFF system incorporated into it. However upon close inspection it can be seen that the short dipole rod for the new IFF set is not fitted into its location mounting clasps, that can be seen clearly on the outer cover plate of the *Quirl*.

This picturesque location of a model "A" FuMG 62 *Würzburg* radar site is in the hills of northern Yugoslavia. Note the amount of barbed wire around the site, a sure sign that partisans are operating in the area. Of note is the camouflage on the dish that is remarkably similar to another model "A" FuMG 62 *Würzburg* illustrated earlier in this publication, but they are certainly not the same radar set. They are not even from the same unit, which might mean that this camouflage was applied at the factory.

Both the photographs on this page are of the same model "D" FuMG 62 *Würzburg*, it is seen here set up next to a typical French road with the single row of trees down each side, a common site in northern France even today. The notation on the back of these photographs tells us that the location is actually just south of the road to Flers a kilometre or so south-west of Falaise, France. Of note on this radar set are the tailor-made canvas covers over all the optics and instrument panels. They are especially of note as they are not a factory produced item, yet they are so well made and fit so precisely.

This overview is of a complete fire control site for the local Flak batteries in this part of the Dutch coast. This fire control site is located a couple of kilometres inland from the North Sea coast, on the outskirts of the small Dutch town of Alphen aan den Rijn. The site is well established, with wooden duckboard paths laid to and from each location. A folded down and covered mobile FuMG 62 *Würzburg* radar set mounted on its Sd.Anh. 104 transportation bogies can be seen close to what appears to be the main entrance gate to the site. The photo has been taken from the roof of one of the accommodation huts attached to the site, and the view also offers us a look at the day-to-day items that are to be found on a base such as this – a glass flagon of wine wrapped in wickerwork and a galvanized wash tub are just two such items.

In this photograph we have a late model "D" FuMG 62 *Würzburg* that at first does not seem out of the ordinary, however upon closer inspection a few peculiarities start to appear. The crew have been issued the latest in double-sided camouflage combat clothing, usually only available to front line troops and even then they were rare and hard to obtain. Then look closely at the base and it becomes clear this is a radar set that is mounted onto a specially converted railway flatbed carriage and is part of a Flak train. The timber shed-like structure they are standing next to is where the electrical generator is installed.

This photograph is of a mobile model "A" FuMG 62 *Würzburg* radar set that has been updated to model "D" standard and the new rotating *Quirl* housing is clearly visible as are the unit's six kill markings in the form of aircraft silhouettes painted in white onto the radar's main dish. What I like here is the human element – if you look closely at the operator's wooden platform you can see that wire mesh has been fixed under it. What has happened here is the crew have turned their radar's base underfloor area into a chicken coop! Also note the pile of breeze blocks (lightweigh concrete hollow cast building blocks) collected from farm buildings in the area, that the crew are going to use to construct a more permanent emplacement for their radar site.

These two pieces of equipment have just been left in this field, due to be turned into a radar site in the next few days. Still fitted with their respective transportation systems, the two fully covered units are, on the left with the trees behind it, a *Richtungshörer* RRH sound locating set with its associated Sd.Anh. 104 transportation twin bogie system and, on the right with the log post in the ground in front of it, is a 200 cm Sw 40 searchlight with its associated Sd.Anh. 204 transportation twin bogie system. With the two units so close together a useful comparison can be made between the Sd.Anh. 104 and the larger Sd.Anh. 204.

Here we have an early model "D" FuMG 62 *Würzburg* with the *Quirl* without the mounting brackets for the upgraded IFF dipole. Having said that, the older design of IFF is not fitted to this unit either. The lack of this refinement does not seem to have lowered the effectiveness of this unit, however, as the main dish has at least 12 kill markings painted on it, in the form of aircraft silhouettes in white.

This is a rare sight to find in a photograph of the period, this radar set is in its emplacement but is equipped with a repeater. If you look in front of the radar set you will see a table and a set of repeater station scopes next to it, and next to them a repeater board for the instrumentation. Also of note is the extended seating at the main radar operator's position, for either a calibration technician or an operator trainee to sit at.

Below: Located close to the Dutch coast in the early summer of 1944 is this permanently emplaced FuMG 62 *Würzburg*. It looks to be in as-new condition, even the canvas tent for the operator is in good condition and that's a rare sight. Of most interest here is the age of the crew – most look to be just out of school, if indeed they are that old, they may well be younger. Indeed it could be said that their clothing looks older than they do.

This is an early model "A" FuMG 62 *Würzburg* that has been up-dated to the very zenith of *Würzburg* technology and has been upgraded with the fitting of the fully upgraded instrumentation and rotating *Quirl*, complete with IFF equipment installation. This is more than can be said for the emplacement of the radar set! The wooden platform has a decidedly home-made look about it, indeed ramshackle is the word that comes to mind. Note the white painted silhouettes of four-engined bombers painted onto the dish, as indication of the kill tally that the unit had achieved.

This is the same radar set as seen on page 38, some time later. The home-made extension to the operator's platform has collapsed, and the improvised chicken coop had already been disassembled. No doubt its previous occupants have been eaten. Of note, both the crew seen here are wearing their issued sports vests with the Nazi eagle emblem printed on the front.

Another permanent location for a radar site in amongst the flat countryside of Holland. This area was regularly flown over by the large formations of Allied bombers on their way to bomb targets in Germany, so was a prime location for German Flak units. Most of the site including the accommodation huts are all manufactured from timber, the one exception is the concrete bunker that forms part of the emplacement's far side wall.

This is a photograph of the same site as above, but later in its career. Whilst the radar is being kept fully operational and in service, we can see here the concrete bunker that formed only part of the original emplacement wall is being extended to form a fully enclosed concrete emplacement for both the radar and its crew. Once finished it will provide protection for the whole fire control unit.

This radar-equipped Flak unit is parading through the streets of Frankfurt as part of Hitler's birthday celebrations on 20th April 1939. The vehicle being over looked in the foreground is a Krupp L3H163 off-road 6X4 truck towing a covered FuMG 62 *Würzburg* fitted with its Sd.Anh. 104 twin bogie transportation system. It in turn is being followed by another truck of the same type and a Horch staff car.

The two photographs on this page are of the same radar set as seen on page 43, it is a model "A" FuMG 62 *Würzburg* that has been up-dated to model "D" standards. It is seen here in its emplacement before it was up-graded to a fully concrete structure. The site was built in Holland near the Dutch town of Hengelo. I have been to this site and it is now surrounded by woodland. What remains of the concrete structures are being used to house either farm equipment or storage for harvested vegetables, depending upon the time of year. The lower photo is a snapshot taken over the parapet of the emplacement wall of part of the radar's dish. By the time this photo was taken the unit had claimed at least three enemy aircraft destroyed.

In this photograph we see an example of the last of the line, a late production model "D" FuMG 62 *Würzburg* complete with the IFF radio sets dipole fitted to the rotating *Quirl* housing. This radar site is located on the Channel coast and that is the reason stated for the elaborate camouflage screen, made of canvas cloth stretched tight and then doped like WWI aircraft wings or theatrical stage sets. They were then painted to resemble a house or barn. The radar could operate from within such structures without to much interference, but the structures were not strong and needed a lot of maintenance. Usually the RAF knew where the radar sites were anyway through radio detection, aerial photography or via information supplied from the local resistance.

Below left: A nice photograph taken as night falls and the main operator starts to power up this early model "D" FuMG 62 *Würzburg* without the IFF system installed and the early cover for the rotating *Quirl*. Depending upon the weather it could take anything between 20 to 30 minutes to warm the set up to peak working efficiency.

Below right: Here we have a great profile of an early model "D" FuMG 62 *Würzburg* without the IFF system installed, mounted on a raised wooden platform in northern Belgium close to the town of Eeklo. This was a common way to see the *Würzburg* installed as in the Low Countries where flooding was common, such an expensive electrical device was best kept off the wet ground. Whilst being raised did slightly improve the clarity of the return signal, it was at the cost of making both the radar and its operating crew vulnerable to any attack. Note the wooden duckboard pathways running from one site facility to another.

This is a good close-up portrait of a radar operator, posing next to the main dish of the early model "D" FuMG 62 *Würzburg* he helped to operate. This view clearly shows the early style enclosure for the radar's rotating *Quirl* and a rare clear view of a kill marking, showing not only the white painted silhouette of either a British Vickers Wellington or a Handley Page Type HP.52 Hampden, but also the date that it had been shot down – 3rd November 1941 – with the assistance of targeting information received from this radar unit.

A good relaxed group photograph of the crew of this FuMG 62 *Würzburg* radar set. The small group seated on the operating platform are repairing a power cable connector that was probably tripped over in the night and had been damaged. Of note is the sign that is written in classical old Germanic text – "*Zutritt Strengstens Verboten*" (Access Strictly Banned). This is poignant as it does go some way to explain why photographs of *Würzburgs* are rare – not only were unauthorised individuals not allowed up close to the radar set, it was also not allowed to photograph the apparatus either. Luckily for us some crew members chose to ignore this order.

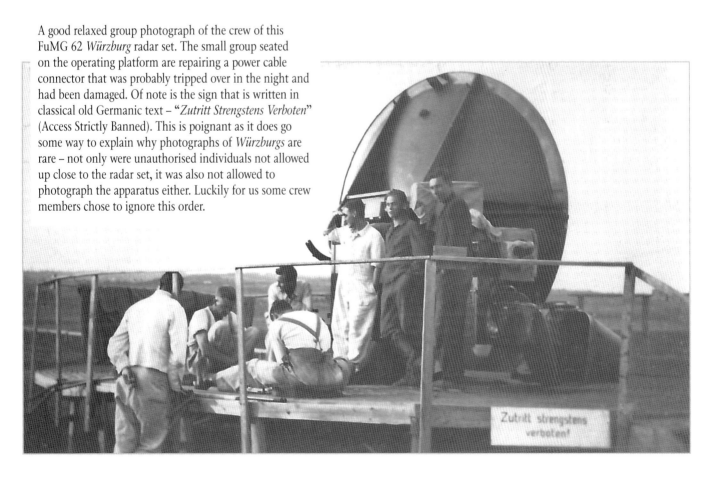

Mobile 24kVA Generator

Photographed in the railway marshalling yard in Frankfurt is this 24-kilowatt, 51-horsepower (38 kW) 8-cylinder engined electrical generator that produced a current of 200 amperes at 110 volts. It was the most common type seen in service with both large searchlight and radar units, and was mounted on a frame that in turn could be coupled to the Sd.Anh. 104 twin bogie transportation system.

A rare and good quality photograph of the ubiquitous Sd.Anh. 104 twin transportation bogies that provided mobility to so many different pieces of German military equipment. They are seen here coupled together so that they could be towed out of the way by one vehicle, once whatever they were being used to transport had been emplaced.

Here we see a *Luftwaffe* unit practising their formation driving in a recently harvested field, for an upcoming parade that they are due to take part in. The trucks seen here towing the electrical generators and associated Sw40 200 cm searchlights are all Henschel D 33s, the most common amongst the types of off-road truck that had been issued to the *Luftwaffe* before 1940.

This is a fantastic close up of an electrical generator that is being prepared for an inspection by its crew, that will take place later in the day. Of note is the flapper topped exhaust at the far right of the photo. This makes this a early example of the type, as the later production units of this type of electrical generator were fitted with an exhaust silencer fixed running horizontally along the centre line of the roof of the generator housing.

This photograph, taken in the garage area of a *Luftwaffe* unit, outside the Panzer Halls (the name given to this type of storage building found in German barracks areas), shows us the type of mobile electrical generator that was used by FuMG 62 *Würzburg* units. However it is seen here with a unit equipped with 150 cm *Flakscheinwerfer* type 37 (150 cm Sw 37) searchlights.

A ship is seen here being loaded with the equipment of a *Luftwaffe* Flak unit and what we see on the docks here are a number of the electrical generators of the type used by FuMG 62 *Würzburg* units. Again they are seen here with a searchlight platoon. Of note is the 150 cm Sw 37 covered searchlight being lifted on-board in the photo, as it offers us a rare top view of the Sd.Anh. 104 twin bogie system as used on many *Würzburgs*.

Here we see an electrical generator belonging to a *Luftwaffe* Flak unit being run up in the field, with its electrical gen-set side of the unit's hatch open. The diesel engine that powered it was located on the other end, behind the closed hatch. The crew member on the right has his hand resting on the lever that will bring the gen-set on load i.e. engage the drive from the motor to the gen-set as soon as the motor is set to run at the required rpm. Note the two main circuit breakers are currently in the off position (the two stirrup shaped handles are both in the down position). Lastly of note in this pre-war photo is that all three of the crew seen here are wearing GM-24 gas masks in the canvas carrying bags, which were issued from 1924. Behind the line units like this would have been the last to be issued with the new masks in their tin tube container with which we are more familiar.

Another gen-set seen whilst powering up, again the crew wait ready to turn the power on as soon as requested to do so. Both the circuit breakers are currently in the off position. Also of interest in both the photos on this page is that both the generators are being operated still mounted to their Sd.Anh. 104s. Note also the way that the crew have stood the kKR98 rifles together to prevent them being just laid on the ground, which was an offence in any army then as it is now.

This gen-set is being towed to its next operating position by a KHD S3000 truck. The emplacement looks to be coastal with sand everywhere, yet two small trees have been cut down to provide camouflage for the gen-set once it is set up. Quite how that camouflage is going to work I am not sure.

Opposite page, top: Both these generator sets are seen here being serviced in their home base motor pool area. One of the main clues that they are not in the field is that none of the field pioneer equipment has been issued or stowed on the Sd.Anh mudguards. The bracket that can be seen in the far right of the photo was for a short handled hatchet/axe and it missing on both gen sets, also of note in this photo we get to see the fire extinguisher fitted in the electrical compartment of the gen-set. It is the tube like item stowed upright against the central support panel of the outer cover of the unit.

Opposite page bottom: This gen-set is tucked under an escarpment for protection. No doubt the equipment it is powering up, be it a searchlight or radar set, will be on the upper edge of the escarpment for a clear field of view. This photo give us the clearest sight of the main switchgear and circuit breakers yet. The four rectangular black box-like items are the circuit trip fuses and the two large black objects with spade (stirrup) handles are the main circuit breakers. We can also see to advantage the fire extinguisher in its stowage bracket. The box like item next to the operator's foot is the diesel engine's battery box.

This operator is adjusting the fuel flow for the diesel motor that is seen to be running by the puffs of exhaust coming out of the exhaust pipe. The diesel's radiator has its cold weather canvas cover in place, yet the gen-set is open due to it just going through its start-up procedure. To the left of the gen-set a 50 meter reel of cable can be seen, usually at least one and sometimes two of these reels were stowed on each of the two halves of the Sd.Anh. 104 twin bogies. This view again gives us a good view of the inner working of this type of mobile gen-set.

I feel cold just looking at this photograph… Here we have a pair of trucks from a *Luftwaffe* radar unit attached to a flak regiment that have slid into each other whilst one was attempting to pass the other. This has happened even though both trucks and loads are clearly fitted with snow chains. The towed loads here are, to the left of the photo an electrical generator and on the right, a FuMG 62 *Würzburg* set. The truck on the left looks as if it collided while trying to overtake.

All packed up waiting to move on, this group of *Luftwaffe* personnel and their associated equipment and provisions are patiently waiting for their assigned transportation to turn up. Due to the lack of motorized transportation, rear echelon units such as radar and searchlight units often had to share transport from other units. As the war progressed as there was never enough transport to go around. Note the good view of the Sd.Anh. 104 and the 100 m reusable reel of high voltage cable in the background, usually associated with units equipped with either the large Sw40 200 cm searchlight or the FuMG 62 *Würzburg* radar.

"Oops" – having slid off the road this Krupp L3H163 off-road 6X4 truck is going to have to be recovered. The crew have all dismounted but none look too eager to get on with the task in hand. I guess the NCO is just telling the crew to uncouple the Gen-set from the truck and get it out of the way before any recovery effort can be made for the truck itself. Note stowed on the Sd.Anh. 104's mudguards an axe on one side and a shovel the other, both standard equipment on each half of the bogie system.

Having just started the diesel engine and while it warms up, the photographer who started the gen-set has left his KR98 leaning up against it and is taking a photo of his charge. Not a glamorous piece of equipment no matter how necessary it was, generator sets were rarely photographed, especially as the hero item in the shot. Note the cable running into the connector box and how it is looped over a forked stick. This was done to give the cable stretch margins so if it was snagged and pulled it would not immediately pull out the cable connector from the socket.

Here we see a crane-barge hoisting an electrical generator onto a ferry just out of view on the other side of the crane barge. Whilst the gen-set is of interest I find the crane barge and the host-rig with its spreader bar just as fascinating, the type of detail that is rarely seen in any publication. The photo was taken in the port of Kiel and the ferry was making the trip to Oslo, Norway.

Opposite page, bottom: This *Luftwaffe* radar unit is seen withdrawing from the Babruysk area in the winter of 1941/42; the infantry who are dug into the frozen mud look on. One can only imagine what thoughts were running through their heads at the sight of the *Luftwaffe* support unit withdrawing from what had probably been their only forward air base that could provide them with air cover. Note the total lack of winter uniforms in evidence here!

This *Luftwaffe* unit is making its way through the Dutch countryside on its way to set up a radar installation on the coast. The unit stopped at this farm overnight and are posing with the farmer's family in the morning before restarting their journey. Not all the Dutch were anti-German at the start of the war, and had the Germans not treated the population so harshly they may well have had another ally, but through misdeeds any support was lost from the vast majority of the Dutch population. However it should be remembered there were many volunteers from Holland that fought for the Germans, there was even a Dutch SS regiment. The gen-set is seen here with Krupp L3H163 6x4 off-road truck.

Left: I feel I should know the location of this city but sadly I do not. However I can tell you that the photograph shows a *Luftwaffe* heavy flak unit on the march. In the background is one of the very rare mobile 128mm flak guns, this must be one of the very first units equipped with the type as the photo was taken in March 1942 and the gun only started production in late December 1941. However the item of interest here is the late production gen-set with the exhaust mounted on the roof of the generator housing, replacing the earlier flapper type end to the exhaust pipe that we have seen in most of the previous photographs in this publication.

Mobile 8 kVA Generator

This type of generator was usually associated with communication units, but they were also working in conjunction with radar units and are often seen sharing the same site with the radar equipment. I have chosen to include a few photographs for your information here, as this type of equipment is not seen in any other publication of note. This is a German Naval communication unit, German Naval units often served with *Luftwaffe* FuMG 62 *Würzburg* Radar units, as the navy had a core of qualified technicians fully trained on the *Würzburg* operating systems but no ships on which to serve.

This great photograph of the 8 kVa electrical generator is a rarity; it offers us a very clear view of the gen-set all set up and in operation. Note the cables running away from the connector box mounted on the trailer frame in the foreground. With all the items in this shot I could go on for ever – empty cable reels, 20 litre jerry cans, electrical connectors and many more things. Suffice it to say all the bits and pieces required to make a working communication site are on view bar the radio sets themselves.

A nice informal pose of two of the NCOs attached to this communications unit next to their Krupp L3H163 Kfz.72 radio communications truck. In the background being towed by this truck is an 8 kVa electrical generator fully packed away for transit.

Bottom: This Faun command and communications truck/caravan is seen in the Norwegian town of Asker, just southwest of Oslo. It is part of an infantry regiment's mobile command and control centre, however we are more interested here in the nice profile view of the 8 kVa electrical generator parked in front of the large truck.

Opposite page, bottom: Here we have an Opel *Blitz* communications truck with a timber cabin that is towing an 8 kVa electrical generator. The latter is seen fully packed away and ready for transportation, in complete contrast to the photo above.

I really like this photograph, it shows a typical workshop truck in service seen in a field in northern France during the invasion of 1940. We can identify a post drill mounted in the back of the truck that also would have contained a lathe and other machine tools. Also seen is a tool box under the rear of the 8 kVa electrical generator and a welding set complete with a welding mask resting on top of it in the foreground. Lastly on the right of the photo is a 500 cc Zundapp motorcycle under repair.

Below: This photo was taken on 9th September 1939 on the training grounds in Luneburg Heath, northern Germany. The truck is a Krupp L3H163 Kfz.72 radio communications vehicle, seen in operation with the 8 kVa electrical generator providing the power. Just visible in the background we can see the telescopic radio mast and some of its guide ropes that hold it in place.